Is Papal Au
a Gift to Us?

A Critique of The Gift of Authority

Colin Buchanan

Bishop of Woolwich

RIDLEY HALL RD CAMBRIDGE CB3 9HU

Contents

1   Introduction 3

2   From The Reformation To Pius IX 5

3   What of 1870? 8

4   Anglicans and Roman Catholics 12

5   Theological Response to *Authority I* and *II* 17

6   ARCIC-2 and *The Gift of Authority* 22

7   Assessing the Claim to Infallibility 28

8   Conclusion 32

     Appendix: How Did It Go So Wrong? 33

     Notes 34

'External force may frighten a man into altering his outward profession, but has no effect on his inward belief. But if he comes to persuade himself of the existence of a guide incapable of leading him wrong, he is ready to surrender his previous beliefs in deference to that authority, to accept as true what he had before proved to be false, and renounce as false what he had before proved to be true...'

(G Salmon, *The Infallibility of the Church*, 2nd ed, 1890, footnote p 23)

First Impression July 2003
ISBN 1 85174 550 5

Introduction 1

The second Anglican-Roman Catholic International Commission (ARCIC-2) published its report on Authority under the title 'The Gift of Authority' on 12 May 1999.[1]

I was involved in controversy about it in the press almost from the day of publication, and my conviction that its theological content and desired outcome are ill-conceived and dangerous will come as no surprise. However, the four years which have elapsed since publication have brought the Church up against a procedural problem which enlarges the problem of content and increases the degree of danger.

I was on the General Synod's Council for Christian Unity when the report was published. For reasons difficult to identify—not all of which arose within or from the CCU and its officers—it has proved impossible to get *The Gift* onto the agenda of Synod in those four years which have elapsed. This is not unprecedented, but is very unhelpful.[2] There exists widespread distrust of the report, but without a debate it remains unfocussed, unmeasured, unreported. Meanwhile, the very existence of such a report, there in print and without a public challenge, starts to give it a standing to which it is not entitled. 'Have not Anglicans and Roman Catholics reached agreement?' is an easy rhetorical question. It affects the atmosphere, for unchallenged reports tend to get quoted as though they had unearthed widespread and substantial accord. There is also the reverse suspicion, that those who want to spread an atmosphere of accord will be tempted to try to postpone gloves-off debate. But here there is surely discord? The unanimous agreement recorded in *The Gift* may, certainly, have been predictable to those who knew *Authority in the Church I* and *II*.[3] But it is deeply prejudicial of the doctrine of biblical authority (and the grounds for separation from Rome) held within the Church of England. ARCIC-2 has laboured for sixteen years, and produced seductively written error.[4]

It is likely, however, that we are now to debate it in February 2003. We have at last some official recognition of its existence, in that the Faith and Order Advisory Group (FOAG) which does theological work for the CCU, produced at the end of 2002 a symposium on the report—Peter Fisher (ed), *Unpacking the Gift: Anglican Resources for Theological Reflection on 'The Gift of*

Authority' (GS Misc 697, Church House Publishing, 2002). The varied papers in the symposium at least testify to *The Gift* being 'controversial' (the key adjective used by Bishop John Hind in the opening paragraph of the Foreword). The lengthy contribution by Martin Davie (one-quarter of the whole symposium) is brutally analytical, and, after discerning many features of *The Gift* which are well said and illuminating, the chapter takes the report apart line by line. My own contribution here is developed from controversy in which I was involved when *The Gift* first came out; it is not dependent upon *Unpacking the Gift*. But it certainly gets support within it;[5] and, cumulatively, *Unpacking the Gift* fires enough ammunition to hole *The Gift* significantly along its whole length below the waterline.

It is fair enough for Christopher Hill to complain that surveying 'the more negative criticisms of *The Gift*' has shown that it 'has not been read in the context of earlier Anglican / Roman Catholic discussions.'[6] As one who shadowed ARCIC-1 rather more closely than I have had the chance to do with ARCIC-2, I take the point. But the way to meet the complaint is to develop history in a sequential way; I have tried to do this, and so establish the context, but it means that *The Gift* itself only comes under the spotlight in the second half of this booklet...

I should slip in my own hope for a genuine convergence of Rome and Canterbury. I am astonished at the progress in my adult lifetime in Christians learning to love each other across a narrowing divide. I have gained much, and also given a little, in those ecumenical birth-pangs. But the simple truth about *The Gift* is that, if I had been a Roman Catholic, I suspect I would have agreed the report gratefully without much ado. To Roman Catholics I have to say only that I hope I have got the history of their Church and its theological position right, and am very sorry if I have not. But it is because I am a slightly knowing Anglican that I have to oppose a report which carries a wrong process to an unwelcome conclusion.

> *ARCIC-2 comes uncommonly close to exactly that which Paul disavows*

Finally, I remark upon the window-dressing of *The Gift*. The Commission commends its work by a repetitive use of 'Yea' and 'Nay,' cited from Paul in 2 Corinthians 1. This will reinforce the credibility of the report to those who like it. But to any who find it ambiguous or doubtful, it is frankly counter-productive to have this stark insistence of 'yes' and 'no' thrust at us throughout. Paul, after all, wrote: 'Our word to you is not "yes" and "no" [*ie* in one breath]' (2 Cor 1.18)—but ARCIC-2 comes uncommonly close to exactly that which Paul disavows. Let the reader decide.

From The Reformation To Pius IX 2

The Powers of the Pope

On the eve of the Reformation the Pope held a patriarchal governing authority over the whole Western Church, and at intervals attempted to bring the Eastern Churches to acknowledge a claim to universal jurisdiction. It was the Pope who dispensed Henry VIII to marry his brother's widow; and a later Pope who entitled him *'Fidei Defensor'* (Defender of the Faith) when Henry wrote against Luther. It was to the Pope that Luther first appealed against indulgences and the sale of pardons; and it was when he discovered that the Pope actually authorized such activities that he left the Pope's jurisdiction. He appealed from the Pope to the Scriptures and the gospel—to clearly stated doctrines to which the papal ecclesial principles were clearly opposed. The Pope in those days was, however, not going in his own person beyond conserving a received system of government and doctrine; and, when the Reformation controversies became too sharp, and the public attacks on the Roman system too loud, the Pope convened the Council of Trent, and it was the Council's part (as had been the case with the Fourth Lateran Council in 1215) to define received doctrine for the counter-reformation purposes. The bishops at Trent did not view themselves as doing other than restating what had been received, resolving ambiguities, facing new issues from known principles, and renewing Canon Law to govern the practice of the church; but definition was the task of a Council. Papal powers were expressed in many ways in the sixteenth and seventeenth centuries, and powerful instances include: the bull which excommunicated Elizabeth in 1570; the enforcement on the continent in 1582 of the Gregorian Calendar; the condemnation in 1615 of a Copernican cosmology (which aimed at Galileo); and the constitution *Unigenitus* in 1713 which outlawed 'Jansenism.' But in these utterances, no Pope ever defined doctrine *ex cathedra* so as to create new credal boundaries and make *de fide* (*ie*, essential to the faith) what had previously been only pious opinion, about which it was still lawful for opinions to differ. Indeed, well-tutored Roman Catholics would deny as defamation any suggestion that they thought the Pope infallible. A classic example of this is in Keenan's *Catechism*.[7] The 1851 edition (with the Scottish bishops' *Imprimatur*) includes in the section 'On Councils' (page 102):

> *Q.* Must not Catholics believe the Pope in himself to be infallible?
>
> *A.* This is a Protestant invention; it is no article of the Catholic faith; no decision of his can oblige, under pain of heresy, unless it be received and enforced by the teaching body; that is, by the bishops of the Church.

I return to Keenan's *Catechism* below.[8] For the moment, I note that Pius IX, Pope from 1846 to 1878, first of all defined a doctrine in his own person, without reference to a Council, and then convened a Council (Vatican I) to adopt the 'Protestant invention' and make it credal.

The Alternative Story in Anglicanism

The Anglican Reformers, in retaining bishops and bolstering the powers of the monarch, constructed their ecclesiology in a top-down manner. Where the Pope had previously ruled, the monarch now must (and the better kings of Israel and Judah provided scriptural models for this). The 'national church' was the unit of decision-taking; and there were hints of the plurality of such units in the reference in Article XXXIV to 'Every particular or national church.' Conciliar decisions did not bind simply by being conciliar ('General Councils…may err, and sometimes have erred…' (Article XXI)), and where the Articles accepted the outcome of Councils (as with the creeds), they did so not on the grounds that Conciliar authorship sufficed, but that the actual text of the creeds could be 'proved by most certain warrants of holy Scripture' (Article VIII). So, while an episcopal frame of government continued from the pre-Reformation era (and was defended strongly over against anabaptists and presbyterians), the trans-national unity of the church was left undefined, save in respect of the negatives, that Councils could not infallibly declare doctrine, and Popes had no power in England. In the Church of England final authority lay (and, arguably, still lies) with the monarch in Parliament against which and from which there was no appeal.[9]

However, Anglicanism expanded across the globe, and other Anglican solutions to church governmental questions inevitably occurred in other parts of the Communion. The Scottish Episcopalians sustained a 'college of bishops' in a semi-underground way when under persecution as Jacobites. And the Americans in 1785 formed a General Convention to draw together the scattered Anglicans of the emergent Union. In the nineteenth century other new models emerged. Selwyn called a diocesan synod, then a General Synod, in New Zealand. Robert Gray, infuriated by Colenso's appeal to the Privy Council in London against Gray's deposition, summoned a General Synod of the 'Church of the Province of South Africa' and 'separated root and branch' from the Church of England. The Church of Ireland, cast loose by the Westminster Parliament in 1870 to become a voluntary association, by mutual bonding formed a General Synod to take authority. The instances could be multiplied, till today there are 38 autonomous provincial (or equivalent) bodies within the Anglican Communion. These have gained enormous advantages in addressing local problems without recourse to the other ends of the earth, and in addressing governing and other powers in their own nations not as dancing on strings pulled from elsewhere, but as prophetic forces within their own countries. The reverse side of this coin is that the resultant worldwide Communion naturally then has to wrestle with issues about its own identity and unity, about how provinces are to act together without any overall constraining authority keeping them in step. The history of international Anglicanism since, say, the first Lambeth Conference in 1867, is one of a deep (and yet not uncritical) sense of all belonging to each other in Christ, and yet of an equal sense of the need to react to the actual context of each province—even if this appears to set one province in tension with others in the Communion. The supreme authority and relative perspicuity of Scripture has in theory remained as the place of final appeal in theology. But in practice provinces, dioceses, and individuals have not only read Scripture differently from each other, but have often fudged or trimmed scriptural teachings for the sake of relating to their own context.

The resultant, no doubt largely accidental, constitution of the Anglican Communion, means that the various provinces have to hold to each other through love and a sense of belonging to each other. If they are to take counsel together, they are convened, as another accident of history, by the Archbishop of Canterbury. They resist any efforts to provide a single worldwide ruling body. They could possibly produce a kind of 'universal primate' from among themselves at the moment (probably the Archbishop of Canterbury), if they were widely convinced it was right to do so. But not only are they ready to remain in their 38 national provinces. It is at least arguable that they have a rough correspondence to the pre-Nicene Church in so doing—and that the degree of honour (which was not obedience) paid to Rome before the Peace of Constantine is little different from the honour (which is not obedience) accorded to Canterbury in today's Anglican Communion. Some of this could have been stated more confidently in *The Gift*.

We are free to rethink our ecclesiology

But, there is an underlying further factor for Anglicans to treasure. It is simply this: we are free to rethink our ecclesiology. We do not have to defend any one decision, one utterance, one constitutional form as somehow being God's final word on a subject. We have freedom to criticize our past, freedom to rethink. Our very growth across the world has required this, and the various provinces have discovered it. It is a freedom Rome lacks.

7

3

What of 1870?

1870 is famous as the year of Vatican I, the point where a Council declared the Pope, when defining doctrine ex cathedra, to be infallible. But the story starts earlier.

Pius IX (1846–78) was the last Pope to rule over the papal states in Italy, and the political and military defeats he suffered are part of the key to his asserting the powers of his office. However, the story can be told largely within the doctrinal field. In 1854 he defined in the bull *Ineffabilis Deus* the Immaculate Conception of the Virgin Mary. This doctrine exhibits a kind of *a priori* argument as follows:

a) Our Lord was free of original sin (like Adam before the Fall);

b) *Ergo* he did not inherit the taint of original sin from his Mother;

c) *Ergo* she was free of the taint herself when she conceived him in her womb;

d) But she had been born of two natural parents who were both heirs to the transmission of original sin;

e) *Ergo* a miracle had occurred at her conception in the womb of her mother (St Anne) which had eliminated the taint of original sin, and in that 'immaculate' conception had freed her from original sin, and qualified her to bear Jesus.

This was indeed a long-held 'pious opinion,' but it was in the category of speculation, and until 1854 it was perfectly consistent with loyalty to the faith, even if rare in practice, to deny or at least question the doctrine. Thomas Aquinas and Torquemada were among the medievals who had most notably denied it.[10] Pius IX now issued the definition—exactly as the Council of Trent (and previous Councils) had done with their doctrinal decrees. It took the form of a conciliar decree; it had all the authority of the Pope; it was, in any case, already widely believed; and it was gloriously confirmed by the miracle of St Bernadette of Lourdes who in 1858 had a vision of the Virgin Mary who was reported to have said, 'I am the Immaculate Conception' (an interesting example of synecdoche). But there still remained a lingering doubt as to whether the Pope had power to issue such an irreversible definition and imposition of doctrine on his own, without any participation by a Council. Certainly readers of Keenan's *Catechism* in the post-1854 years must have occasionally wondered who was actually engaged in 'invention.'[11]

However, all was to be quickly resolved. The Pope convened a General Council for late 1869 in the Vatican. The major question was whether the Pope could pronounce on doctrine *ex cathedra* beyond any question of error, even without the presence, consultation and voting of a General Council. If Vatican I could so state, then papal infallibility would not need to be part of a circular argument, but would rest on a conciliar basis—though, on the other hand, it could well be that no General Council would ever be needed again. The question was perceived as a cross-roads in Roman Catholic history; and a few bishops declined to attend the Council lest they be implicated in a decision-taking process of which they did not approve—turning the 'Protestant invention' into Catholic truth. Opposition at the Council took a different, somewhat subdued, form—not that papal infallibility was untrue or even doubtful, but that it was 'inopportune' to impose it as an article of the faith. At the Council itself, even as troops closed in on the city of Rome and the last papal state was wrenched from the Vatican's grasp, only two inopportunists among over 600 bishops present voted against the decree (though over 50 abstained). Outside the Council, however, all was not so peaceable. In Germany Dollinger and half a million clergy and laity left and became 'Old Catholics.' Bishops who had boycotted the Council wriggled under the new pressure before conforming. Protestant controversialists took up their pens to quote pre-Vatican I utterances of leading Roman Catholics against their novel subscription to the formula. And Keenan's *Catechism* smoothly changed its line. Thus my 1896 edition (revised by a new editor) has on its comparable page 118 an identical set of surrounding questions, but within the set the one answered by 'Protestant invention' is missing. Instead, at an earlier point (in the section 'On the Head of the Church' on page 112) there is a question about infallibility, then a further question about how at an earlier point it had been possible for Catholics (and indeed earlier editions of Keenan's *Catechism* itself) to deny the infallibility—and the answer was that, even whilst explicitly denying it, they were 'implicitly' asserting it.

The actual text of the crucial part of the 1870 decree ran as follows:

> The definitions of the Roman pontiff (speaking *ex cathedra*) are irreformable of themselves and not by virtue of the Church's consent...[12]

The Latin original had '...*ex sese, non ex consensu*...' Nothing could be clearer—and thus it gave the retrospective infallibility to the Immaculate Conception decree. The phraseology has been subjected to all kinds of maximizing and minimizing, but there are severe limits to its stretchability, and it is unequivocally *there* in all Roman Catholic thought since 1870. Thus Vatican II pronounced:

> The Roman pontiff...enjoys this infallibility in virtue of his office, when, as supreme pastor and teacher of all the faithful...he proclaims in an absolute decision a doctrine pertaining to faith and morals.[13]

In 1870 the definition was intended to be followed by further definitions of conciliar powers, affirming the corporate role of the episcopate; but, because of the military situation, the Council was disbanded before it reached the rest of the agenda on authority. This omission hardly bears upon papal infallibility, as the text above so clearly relates to the Pope issuing statements or definitions on his own, independently of any Council. It is exactly that infallibility which is in question in this assessment of *The Gift*.

However, Vatican I did not give birth (as it might have) to a string of new definitions coming at intervals over the years. There has only been one *ex cathedra* definition since 1870—the decree on the Bodily Assumption of our Lady into heaven (1950). This decree obviously derives from the 1854 one concerning the Immaculate Conception. The logical argument set out in (a) to (e) on page 8 above is now extended as follows:

> e) ...a miracle had occurred at Mary's conception in the womb of her mother (St Anne) which had eliminated the taint of original sin, and in that 'immaculate' conception had freed her from original sin, and qualified her to bear Jesus.
>
> f) *Ergo*, because she was not tainted by sin, her body was not subject to corruption and her person not liable to death, and so, when the right number of her years had passed, she was 'assumed' [*ie* 'taken up'] into heaven bodily, without passing through death.

This doctrine also had been gradually adopted during the history of the church. It is not attested in extant literature before the late fourth century; and was apparently first given respectable credibility by Gregory of Tours towards the end of the sixth century. The belief in it had become almost universal among Roman Catholics by the twentieth century, and Pope Pius XII took considerable steps to verify its widespread acceptance before 'defining' the doctrine (and he obviously reckoned he was 'defining' what was already believed, rather than imposing what was not). Nevertheless the definition made the belief for the first time *de fide*, and helped to present a controversial Roman Catholic front to the rest of the Christian world. It also aired the exercise of the *ex cathedra* infallibility for the first time since it had been defined.

I do not here attempt to refute these two Marian definitions (by biblical standards they are very doubtful indeed—and were on those grounds dropped from the Church of England calendar in 1549). They are at best speculative, at worst erroneous and even harmful (as they elevate the Virgin Mary too high above sinful humanity, and do so not because of scriptural warrant but because of a kind of doctrinal or devotional auction down history). Anglicans may believe these doctrines or not as private opinions, but they cannot conceive that they are *de fide*, integral to the creed of Christians, indispensable and central to a true faith. At any rate, these two together are 'The Marian decrees' and are from now on so denominated when the two of them together are in view; and, although one preceded 1870 and one followed it, they comprise together the sole acknowledged exercise of the *ex cathedra* powers, and form together a kind of test case of that exercise.

Anglicans cannot conceive that these doctrines are indispensable and central to a true faith

I should add, what I have already adumbrated in the Introduction, that in the 1950s, while we might have expected further *ex cathedra* definitions, the one thing we were sure could never happen again, now the Pope's powers were so secured, was that a Council should be convened. But we had reckoned without John XXIII…

4   Anglicans and Roman Catholics

From 1833 to 1960

From the start of the Oxford Movement in 1833, there had been Anglicans (of an 'advanced' Catholic persuasion) who had sought a reconciliation of the two Communions. These hopes grew as the Movement expanded; but they were of course dashed by the Vatican I definition. Pusey, who in the mid-1860s had been optimistic about his *Eirenicon* (a dealing with obstacles to the reunion of Anglicans with Rome), published just before the Vatican Council a sequel in the form of a letter written to Newman *Is Healthful Reunion Impossible?* This was followed in 1876 by a further letter to him, now entitled *Healthful Reunion, as conceived possible before the Vatican Council*, the very title betraying the sense of frustration at the near-impossibility of achieving that which had seemed to him a realistic aim prior to Vatican I. The atmosphere was never helped by the attitude of English Roman Catholics (some of them, like Manning, ex-Anglicans), who were totally opposed to recognizing any marks of ecclesial orthodoxy in Anglicanism. Their policy was, by making no concessions, to maximize on individual 'conversions,' and keep the sharpest possible contrast between the one true Church, and the Anglican schism and heresy. The matter was vividly illustrated when Lord Halifax, a redoubtable lay Anglo-Catholic leader, was engaged in the 1890s in informal conversations with the Abbé Portal in Belgium. This led to denunciations of the process by English Roman Catholics, and in turn led to the condemnation of Anglican Orders by Leo XIII in 1896. This encyclical, *Apostolicae Curae*, was obviously intended to end all hopes of Anglicans of getting somewhere with the Pope *as Anglicans*. Instead they had to recognize the only safe and proper way of being 'Catholics' was to submit outright to Rome and become properly Roman Catholics. The encyclical was not itself infallible, but, in the juridical and administrative capacity of the Pope, it purported to close the question for all time.[14]

The matter was resumed in 1921, when the same Lord Halifax, now in his eighties, with same Abbé Portal, started some 'unofficial' conversations at Malines in Belgium. They notified the Pope and the Archbishop of Canterbury, and were accorded a kind of recognition which meant that 'the Malines Conversations' are an identifiable exercise in Church history. They lasted from 1921 to 1926, when Portal died. Then, after a delay, Halifax published the documents; but the exercise had ceased. It was, perhaps, most notable for the paper by Lambert Beauduin 'L'Eglise d'Angleterre unifié non absorbée.' This outlined a (hypothetical) process by which the Church of England would be united with the Church of Rome on a 'Uniat' basis, keeping some or all of its distinctive culture (vernacular liturgy, married priesthood?), but in ultimate submission, as a corporate ecclesial body, to the Pope.[15] The whole Malines process was denounced by many in the Church of England and was ruled out of order by Pius XI in the very ruthless banning of conversations in *Mortalium Animos* in January 1928.

Vatican II and the Founding and Agreements of ARCIC-1

John XXIII became Pope at the age of 77 in 1958. Within a few months, he announced that he was convening a General Council—though for pastoral, not doctrinal, reasons. This Council would not make doctrinal definitions—and it did not. It met from Autumn 1962 to Autumn 1965, and it produced a great series of Decrees, statements of general principle about the life and conduct of the Roman Catholic Church. This included the Decree on Ecumenism (*Unitatis redintegratio*, 1964), and warmed the atmosphere for relationships between Roman and Anglicans. Michael Ramsey met with John XXIII's successor, Paul VI, in 1966, and there emerged the first Anglican Roman Catholic International Commission (ARCIC-1). ARCIC-1 produced agreed Statements on the Eucharist (1971) and on Ministry and Ordination (1973). Then came two separate Statements on Authority, *viz*, *Authority in the Church I* (1976) and *Authority in the Church II* (1981). The whole set of Statements, including 'Elucidations' in relation to the Eucharist, Ministry and Ordination, and *Authority in the Church I*, was published in *The Final Report* (CTS/SPCK, 1982).

The *Authority* Statements were not intended at the time to be either exhaustive or fully agreed. They reckoned to take agreement as far as was possible, and then to chart the ground where there was disagreement. In the process *Authority I* recorded the following agreements:

1 There are some initial fairly brief and lightweight affirmations about the authority of the written Scriptures and of the Holy Spirit in the church.

2 About bishops, they affirm in the ordained ministry a pastoral authority. 'This pastoral authority belongs primarily to the bishop... Since the bishop has general oversight of the community, he can require the compliance necessary to maintain faith and charity in its daily life.'

3   They assert a universal primacy, as exemplified in the teaching of Vatican I and II. The primacy is there 'to guard and promote the faithfulness of all the churches to Christ and one another.' In other words, it is a key instrument of the worldwide unity and communion of the church.

4   In matters of faith they accord a key role to councils and 'The bishops are collectively responsible for defending and interpreting the apostolic faith.' But the responsibility of individual bishops for clarifying and defending the faith provides a pattern which 'needs to be realized at the universal level.' A *locus* at Rome for the bishop at this universal level is claimed on the grounds that Rome is the only place in the world to have made such a claim.

After this come points not yet agreed by Anglicans in relation to the Pope. These are listed at the end of *Authority I* and become the agenda for *Authority II*.

1   The 'Petrine texts'—how much weight can they bear?

2   The status of Vatican I's attribution of 'divine right' to the papal office.

3   The claim of infallibility, and thus 'special difficulties...created by the recent Marian decrees.'

4   The assertion of 'universal immediate jurisdiction, the limits of which are not clearly specified.'

After *Authority I* was published in 1976, the Commission addressed the responses to all the Statements published by then and issued *'Elucidations'* on all three, that on *Authority I* in 1981. In this *Elucidation* they addressed seven topics from *Authority I*:

1   'The Place of Scripture.' Here the Commission propounds both a tradition which 'is primarily concerned never to go beyond the bounds of Scripture' and one which is somewhat wider—and neither tradition has the seal of truthfulness upon it prior to 'reception by the whole Church.'

2   'Councils and Reception.' Here the Commission emphasizes that Councils are only preserved from error when they are enunciating 'fundamental matters of faith' which are 'faithful to Scripture and consistent with tradition.' They discuss the status of 'reception' of such formulations, trying to keep a narrow line between affirming that Councils get it right quite independently of any re-

ception, and affirming that a formulation really has no standing until it has been 'received.'

3 'The Place of the Laity.' The Commission thought it had been accused of neglecting the laity. In two brief paragraphs it 'elucidates' that every layperson should carry out the particular function that baptism gives to each. Both Churches have sought ('sometimes hesitantly') to integrate lay people in decision-taking. It had only been reticent on 'The Place of the Laity' because it was about ordained people that difficulties had appeared to exist. Lay people include those with special gifts, and all have a part in the reception process, and in bearing witness.

4 'The Authority of the Ordained Ministry.' They have been criticized for saying that a bishop has authority 'to require compliance.' They simply defend the power concerned.

5 'Jurisdiction.' There is a short further elucidation of powers concerned.

6 'Regional Primacy.' They are ready to affirm some form—and various possible forms—of regional primacy.

7 'Primacy and History.' They argue that the claim of Rome as the see for universal primacy is 'more than historical.' They demonstrate how Anglicans both value primacy already and will gain by adopting a universal primacy—though the argument is not based greatly on projected advantages but on a more-or-less revealed doctrinal necessity.

In *Authority II*, also in 1981, the four points raised in *Authority I* for further treatment are addressed as follows.

On the **Petrine texts**, yes, Peter was leader among the apostles; but 'The New Testament contains no explicit record of a transmission of Peter's leadership.' Ah, but in history 'the church at Rome...came to be recognized as possessing a unique responsibility among the churches.' The Petrine texts show that Peter's relationship to the other apostles provides an 'analogy' for the role of the Bishop of Rome among his fellow bishops.[16]

The fear about *'divine right'* arose from an Anglican understanding that Rome was teaching that not to be in communion with the Pope was not to be a church at all. However, as Rome has recognized the Orthodox Churches *as* churches and has a more modified teaching now about the nature of the church, that fear has diminished. Thus 'we believe that the primacy of the bishop of Rome can be affirmed as part of God's design for the universal *koinonia* in terms which are compatible with both our traditions. Given such consensus, the language of divine right used by the First Vatican Council need no longer be seen as a matter of disagreement between us.'

The issue of *jurisdiction* is handled next, although it was number 4 in the *Authority I* Statement (and is possibly promoted to leave the most difficult of all—infallibility—till last). Jurisdiction is first the decision-taking powers of a bishop—any bishop—in relation to his own diocese. Although said not to be an 'arbitrary power,' it does appear to be exercised without much appeal or accountability (except to the universal primate). In other words, it is a very Roman concept of the episcopate. It is then used as an analogy for advocating comparable universal powers for the universal primate. These are stated in strong language and are there to 'enable him to further catholicity.' In the last analysis, it seems he is himself the one who decides what will 'further catholicity.' Anglicans, we are told, need assurance 'that the acknowledgment of the universal primacy of the bishop of Rome would not involve the suppression of…traditions which they value or the imposition of wholly alien traditions.' Ah, but the signatories say that their own formulations now provide grounds for such assurance.

Infallibility comes fourth. Both councils and universal primates have engaged down history in an exercise of doctrinal authority when they 'have protected legitimate positions which have been under attack.' However, the issue has to come particularly to the Pope: 'A service of preserving the Church from error has been performed by the bishop of Rome as universal primate both within and outside the synodal process.' This much is stated in para 29 as simply agreed on both sides.[17] But since Vatican I the Pope has had powers which Anglicans may well distrust. *Authority II* states that Anglicans would want to examine any *ex cathedra* papal statement on its merits, not being ready (one assumes) simply to accept it from *a priori* convictions about the Pope's capacities. They cite 'the reaction of many Anglicans to the Marian definitions.' The key link is:

> For many Anglicans the teaching authority of the bishop of Rome, independent of a Council, is not recommended by the fact that through it these Marian doctrines were proclaimed as dogmas binding upon the faithful. Anglicans would also ask whether, in any future union between our two Churches, they would be required to subscribe to such dogmatic statements.

A good question. Do those Anglicans have an answer in *The Gift*?

Theological Response to Authority 1 and 11

The Church of England Response

It was clear, from the moment ARCIC-1 began making statements on Authority, that they left more issues open than the other Statements did. When *The Final Report* came to the Church of England in the mid-1980s, we were asked to support the eucharistic and ministry/ordination Statements as being 'consonant in substance with the faith of the Church of England.' But the official Synod motion about the Authority Statements was different:

> That this Synod recognizes that [the Statements] record sufficient convergence on the nature of authority in the Church for our communions together to explore further the structures of authority and the exercise of collegiality and primacy in the Church.

This looks more cautious, but it still rang warning bells. The Authority Statements centred on how far the bishops hold corporate responsibility for governing the church and sustaining its doctrinal orthodoxy—and how far the right kind of universal primate would take over such corporate responsibility. Yet the Commission's Anglicans had agreed a universal primacy based at Rome; they had virtually agreed that the authority they sought already resides in the existing Bishop of Rome; and they had only jibbed minimally at the concept of 'infallibility,' with a minor concern that Anglicans might ask further questions before agreeing that the Marian decrees were integral to the faith—were *de fide*. Now the Commission had affirmed that nothing should be taught which is not scriptural, but had apparently left to Councils or Popes themselves the role of deciding that their own formulations are scriptural. On this basis, could any Luther or Cranmer who had agreed these sort of Statements ever have been involved in challenging contemporary church teaching as being unscriptural? The rug would have been out from under their feet. A Reformation would have been simply impossible.

Thus the Authority Statements, far from 'recording sufficient convergence,' were actually subversive of almost every reason there might ever have been—or might currently be—for a world denomination to stand separate from Rome. The outcome relates to the procedure followed. Clearly the agenda had been set by Roman Catholics saying 'Surely you can accept a papacy, if we can divest the institution of its worst ultramontane accretions'?[18] Thus the issue about authority became, almost as a first move 'What kind of universal primate can we agree on; and what would be the powers of other bishops—individually and together?' This kind of agenda-setting reveals a dynamic on the Commission—one to which I return in the Appendix—which in effect placed the Roman system on the table at the outset, and then said to the Anglicans 'We may find we can recommend some small adjustments which will bring you in in agreement.' Those who stand back from such dynamics can see that, if it had been the Anglicans who had been able and willing to make the pre-emptive strike, then the Commission might have been facing different questions, such as:

1   How can the Scriptures best judge, correct and reform the church?

2   How can the laity be treated as a serious part of the decision-making processes of the church, with popes, prelates, and potentates brought properly to account before the bar of Scripture?

Questions such as these might have been very difficult for the Church of Rome to hear. But surely the Roman programme, which the Commission in fact addressed, should have been equally difficult for Anglicans to address? If it was not, was that because the Anglican members started off less committed to any one pattern than the Roman Catholics, and less bound to defend their own history in quite the way Roman Catholics are? At any rate, the Roman question prevailed, and, in a Commission where friendships were strengthening over many years, the Anglicans found themselves giving ever more compliant answers. What then happens (and I have seen this with other Commissions) is that, when one side responds to agenda set by the other side by invisibly giving ground a fraction more each time they meet, they find themselves at the end commending a position they did not hold at the beginning, and one to which their friends who have been outside the process find they cannot easily accede.

The concept of 'convergence' really meant that those who agreed it were accepting the goal of a universal primate, located in Rome, with some questions to work out about the relative location of powers as between Pope and bishops, and some issues to solve in relation to 'infallibility.' I found myself quite unable to accept that goal, and thus always voted against the motion that there was 'sufficient convergence' for us to go further down the same path.[19] I was not alone; the General Synod handled the main motion, noted on the previous page on the Authority Statements on 13 November 1986. It was then passed by the following majorities: Bishops 38–5; Clergy 182–43;

Laity 124–89. It is clear that the figure in the House of Laity reflects considerable unease about the place of the laity within the Authority Statements.

The Synod then passed a motion about the whole of *The Final Report*, saying that it 'offers a sufficient basis for taking the next concrete steps towards the reconciliation of our Churches,' and that was passed much more easily. There were then private members' following motions and two of these, both passed easily on a show of hands without any speeches opposing, are worth recording also.

That this Synod requests that in the continuing search for Agreement on Authority in the Church particular attention be given to the place and role of the laity, clergy and bishops in the exercise of authority.

That this Synod

a) welcomes the recognition [in documents before it] that in carrying further the ARCIC discussion on Authority 'there are a number of points on which work is needed';

b) records its own conviction that for 'the next concrete steps towards the reconciliation of our churches' [from the resolution quoted above] to make real progress they must include as a matter of priority:

i) a proper recognition of the place of the laity in the decision-making processes and ministry of the whole body of the church;

ii) a more adequate treatment of the Roman Catholic Marian and Infallibility dogmas; and

iii) further attention to the case for a universal primacy necessarily based at Rome, including the official Roman Catholic claim that the Pope is the Vicar of Christ on earth, and accordingly

c) directs that this resolution be conveyed [together with others] to the World Council of Churches and the Anglican Consultative Council

The Lambeth Conference Response

At the 1988 Lambeth Conference, the section report on Ecumenical Relations was very thin on the Authority Statements.[20] This is the resolution which came for adoption in plenary:

This Conference:

[1 concerned the other Statements]

2 Welcomes the assurance that, within an understanding of the Church as communion, ARCIC-2 is to explore further the particular issues of…continuing questions of authority, including the relation of Scripture to the Church's developing Tradition and the role of the laity in decision-making within the Church.

3 Welcomes *Authority in the Church* (*I* and *II*) together with the *Elucidation*, as a firm basis for the direction and agenda of the continuing dialogue on authority and wishes to encourage ARCIC-2 to continue to explore the basis in Scripture and Tradition of the concept of a universal primacy, in conjunction with collegiality, as an instrument of unity, the character of such primacy in practice, and to draw upon the experience of other Christian Churches in exercising primacy, collegiality and conciliarity.

[4 concerned the ordination of women, and 5 was a welcome to the first report from ARCIC-2, *Salvation and the Church* (1987)][21]

I spoke against this resolution, on the grounds that the major question being handled in the Statements named in part 3 was simply that of the relative powers of papacy and episcopate, with no place at all in decision-making for the laity—so the Statements gave *no* acceptable 'direction and agenda.' They were going in a wrong 'direction.' The resolution went through on a show of hands without a count.[22] It is odd that, although the place of the laity was mentioned in part 2 (and just possibly in the 'collegiality' and 'conciliarity' terminology in part 3[23]), the Marian decrees got no mention anywhere at all in the resolution—nor indeed anywhere in the Conference Report.

The Vatican Response

Following the not-quite-official 'Observations' of the Congregation of the Doctrine of the Faith in the 1980s, the definitive papal response came in 1991.[24] It was in this response that the Vatican raised such profound doubts about the language used of the eucharist and ordination by ARCIC-1 as to lead ARCIC-2 into a set of glosses to assuage those doubts, glosses aimed entirely and overtly for consumption by Rome, in their document *Clarifications* (1993). It is hardly surprising that the Vatican had similar worries about *Authority I* and *II*, but in this case, as a whole set of questions had already been remitted to ARCIC-2 by those statements, no emergency one-sided document was needed. All would come in due course. And, of course, because the ARCIC-1 statements had already gone a long way in Rome's direction, Rome did not have to say anything about, for example, the place of the laity in decision-taking. As far as the Marian decrees are concerned, the response says simply that there is 'need for much further study to be done in respect of the petrine ministry in the Church'—in other words, if we get the Pope's authority right, we shall find the Marian decrees follow *as a consequence* (and independently of any enquiry or study about Mary). We can thus see coming the handling of infallibility.

The heart of the criticism here is to be found in this quotation:

> [The statement does sometimes clearly state that truth is dispensed by authority prior to reception] But... it would seem that elsewhere the Final Report sees 'the assent of the faithful' as required for the recognition that a doctrinal decision of the Pope or of an Ecumenical Council is immune from error (*Authority II*, paras 27 and 31). For the Catholic Church, the certain knowledge of any defined truth is not guaranteed by the reception of the faithful that such is in conformity with Scripture and Tradition, but by the authoritative definition itself on the part of the authentic teachers.[25]

That is crystal clear. The authority teaches truth irreformably. No-one can question it. It is in conformity with Scripture and Tradition because the authority says so. *Causa finita est.*

That was the agenda-setting to which ARCIC-2 had to conform. Perhaps we should have seen its answers coming.

6 ARCIC-2 and The Gift of Authority

ARCIC-2 had a task in respect of Authority bequeathed from ARCIC-1 from its outset in 1983. Their work on the unresolved issues led to their fully agreed Statement, *The Gift*, published on 12 May 1999. They cautioned (as all Commissions must) that their report was 'not an authoritative declaration by either the Anglican Communion or the Roman Catholic Church'—no, it was an agreement simply of the Commission members. But it was continuing the 'direction' set by *Authority I* and *II*, and was overtly handling the issues left unresolved in 1981. And, we may note in passing, it had taken *sixteen years* for the new Commission to reach a published mind. Some of that time, of course, may have been spent waiting for Anglican synods, the 1988 Lambeth Conference and the Vatican to make their responses, but the issues were there from the outset, and even 1991 was eight years prior to the Statement being issued. And it seems fair to say that the Commission did indeed follow the 'direction' set by ARCIC-1, and did reach the conclusions to which that direction pointed. In *The Gift* they set out in paragraph 52 the 'Advances in Agreement' which they have registered as follows:

> ...we have deepened and extended our agreement on:
> - how the authority of Christ is present and active in the Church when the proclamation of God's 'Yes' calls forth the 'Amen' of all believers (paragraphs 7–18);
> - the dynamic interdependence of Scripture and the apostolic Tradition and the normative place of Scripture within Tradition (paragraphs 19–23);
> - the necessity of constant reception of Scripture and Tradition, and of re-reception in particular circumstances (paragraphs 24–26);
> - how the exercise of authority is at the service of personal faith within the life of the Church (paragraphs 23, 29, 49);
> - the role of the whole people of God, within which, as teachers of the faith, the bishops have a distinctive voice in forming and expressing the mind of the Church (paragraphs 29–30);
> - synodality and its implications for the communion of the whole

people of God and of all the local churches as together they seek to follow Christ who is the Way (paragraphs 34–40);

- the essential cooperation of the ministry of *episcope* and the *sensus fidei* of the whole Church in the reception of the Word of God (paragraphs 29, 36, 43);

- the possibility, in certain circumstances, of the Church teaching infallibly at the service of the Church's indefectibility (paragraphs 41–44);

- a universal primacy, exercised collegially in the context of synodality, as integral to *episcope* at the service of universal communion; such a primacy having always been associated with the Bishop and See of Rome (paragraphs 46–48);

- how the ministry of the Bishop of Rome assists the ministry of the whole episcopal body in the context of synodality, promoting the communion of the local churches in their life in Christ and the proclamation of the gospel (paragraphs 46–48);

- how the Bishop of Rome offers a specific ministry concerning the discernment of truth (paragraph 47).

I judge that, from this list, we can identify four main issues which have been raised by *Authority I* and *II* and by the response to them in the Church of England and at the 1988 Lambeth Conference. I set them out in order, but it will be clear they rank not only as substantial issues, but also raise a question about the dynamics and procedures of ARCIC-2, comparable to that which I raised on page 18 above about ARCIC-1. In the starkest terms the four issues are:

1 The authority of Scripture;
2 The place of the laity in the structure of the Church;
3 Universal primacy;
4 Infallibility.

1 The Authority of Scripture

The summary above includes about Scripture: 'the dynamic interdependence of Scripture and the apostolic Tradition and the normative place of Scripture within Tradition (paragraphs 19–23).' It must be acknowledged that some very positive statements are made about Scripture, though there is an initial warning note to the discerning in the very words 'normative place of Scripture *within* Tradition' (italics mine). These are echoing, in shorter form, the opening words of para 19: 'Within Tradition the Scriptures occupy a unique and authoritative place and belong to what has been given once for all.' To set a contrast with that slightly weaselly word 'within,' I cite the first 'side' of the Lambeth Quadrilateral: 'The Holy Scriptures of the Old and New Testaments, as "containing all things necessary to salvation," and as being the rule and ultimate standard of faith.' Scripture is not set 'within' Tradition by this phraseology; Tradition is not mentioned as a doctrinal player at all, so it would be fair to say that by this stark phraseology Scripture is set 'over' tradition. *The Gift* goes on talking about 'the Apostolic Tradition,' by which it seems to mean a body of truth not only consolidating what is in Scripture, but also wider than it. If, of course, it only means 'Scripture' by the phrase, it is a great pity it did not say so. For it is a distinguishing of Scripture from Tradition that is needed by Anglicans, not a sinking of the one 'within' the other, which clouds clarity and exposes us to error.

The clue to what is coming is found early in the next chapter: 'By their *sensus fidei* the faithful are able in conscience to recognize God at work in the bishop's exercise of authority' (para 36). The bishops teach—the rest receive. So then the real test of what *The Gift* is saying about Scripture is to be found in paras 41–44 (headed 'Perseverance in the Truth: The Exercise of Authority in Teaching') and here a great plethora of quotations might be adduced. Fairly typical is this 'Doctrinal definitions are received as authoritative in virtue of the divine truth they proclaim as well as because of the specific office of the person or persons who proclaim them within the *sensus fidei* of the whole people of God' (para 43). This appears to say that doctrine is believed first of all because it is taught by people in authority, and then because it is recognized as divine truth. But, one has to say, if the starting point is that the 'Apostolic Tradition' comes to us by a divinely appointed teaching authority, then it is almost certain that that which the authority defines will be recognized as divine truth simply because the authority has defined it; and the hint that the recognition of divine truth is a separate confirmatory procedure is nullified. Why could not the statement say 'Doctrinal definitions are received as authoritative, if, as and when they can be separately verified from the Scriptures, independently of their assertion by people holding specific office'?

A similar characteristic is to be found in the section on primacy: 'In solemnly formulating such [universally required] teaching, the universal primate must discern and declare, with assured assistance and guidance of the Holy Spirit, in fidelity to Scripture and Tradition, the authentic faith of the whole Church, that is, the faith proclaimed from the beginning' (para 47). But the very question an Anglican must ask—one doubly provoked by the Marian decrees to which we return here shortly—is being sidetracked by this kind of statement. We are learning from this sentence that, when the universal primate speaks, he will able to assert that he has the guidance of the Spirit, the mind of the Scriptures, and a continuity with the faith that has been proclaimed through history—and we shall not be able to question it, for it is inbuilt to his speaking at all. The question as to whether, on comparison with Scripture, any such assertion by the universal primate is in fact to be reckoned as consonant with Scripture, is put beyond our power to present. All is well; all is right; all is authoritative; all is to be believed; indeed, all is scriptural—we know that to be the case, for the universal primate has spoken it.

2 The Place of the Laity in the Decision–making Structures of the Church

In para 3 *The Gift* says that the authorities in the two communions have asked for further exploration in three fields, of which the second is 'Collegiality, conciliarity, and the role of the laity in decision-making.' The exploration comes in chapter 3, where 'synodality' is discussed in paras 34–40. It is no twisting of the thrust of these paragraphs to say that the real argument within them is that of *Authority I* and *II*, that is whether the Pope or the bishops as a body (say, in Council) have the last say in decision-taking. Any mention of the laity as having a say comes in para 39, where Anglican existing practices are described. Laity in the Church of Rome are mentioned in para 36 (where 'the faithful' recognize 'God at work in the bishop's exercise of authority'); they are 'consulted' in para 38, but immediately after the bishops 'determine what is to be taught as faithful to the Apostolic Tradition'; and the final *reductio* of what is meant by 'synodality' is reached in para 40 where various forms of bishops' meetings, and of the Pope's meetings with bishops, become what provides 'collegial synodality.' The laity are nowhere in sight, until we are told that 'a growth in synodality at local level is promoting the active participation of lay persons in the life and mission of the local church.' But what this growth is or amounts to does not appear. It remains usually invisible.[26] And, even if it were universal, its 'active participation' does not seem to amount to 'decision-taking.' This particular Anglican question seems to have been brushed aside with this one-line throwaway.

3 Universal Primacy

If the 'direction' of *Authority I* and *II* is to be followed, we are indeed looking for a universal primacy. For my own part, I would not rule it out. However, the concept is not univocal, and it is the unpacking what is meant which will determine whether the quest is worth pursuing. I note the following issues to be resolved:

i) A mere convenor of meetings or an absolute dictator? The powers of a metropolitical archbishop in an Anglican province are usually considerably less than those of a diocesan bishop in his own diocese; and the concept of his 'intervening' is correspondingly hard to focus. On the other hand a Pope at the moment has something near to dictatorial powers. For a universal primate to be accepted, a careful look at the powers would be needed.

ii) A truly synodical, or simply arbitrary, universal primate? If the discussion above about the sidelining of the laity in Roman Catholic power structures is taken seriously, then a universal primate would, presumably, need a worldwide synod—and regular meetings. There are genuine problems in enabling representative laypeople to fulfil such a role—and still be properly participatory laypeople in their own locality. To turn them into professional Vatican-dwellers would achieve nothing.

iii) A doctrinal necessity, or an added bonus? In other words, is this universal primacy of the *esse* or of the *bene esse* of the church of God? If it is of the *esse*, then Anglicans are going to need a lot of teaching—for we had not yet noticed it. But if it is of the *bene esse*, we need to be shown how much better life is with a Pope than without one. That in turn may come to depend upon the answers to the other questions.

iv) A national or an international spokesperson? It may be argued that, when Anglicans speak out against, say, political oppression in their country, they are recognized as speaking from within that country, whereas, when Roman Catholics do, there may well be a suspicion that they are dancing on strings that are being pulled elsewhere. So the question would then be, how is the church best organized for prophetic confrontation with its nation's rulers? But it is possible to respond that a national organization runs the risk of being subverted by its local nationalisms, and an international organization can rise above national interest and be more proof against such subversion. I think this remains a genuinely open question—and its answer may also be bound in with the projected powers of the universal primate.

v) At Rome, or elsewhere? *Authority II* and *The Gift* seem clear that it is the Bishop of Rome who will be the universal primate. One has to say that this jumps a very long way in the argument. The 'Petrine texts,' themselves now somewhat downplayed, obviously do not have Jesus locating Peter at Rome, and Peter's role in Rome, shadowy as it is, has an element of the contingent to it. If, of course, all that happened in the first century is dignified with the adjective 'providentially,' then Rome gets some status thereby. But, even then, it is arguable that, just as the early church's missionary strategy seems to have been to locate the church in cities, from where the gospel would spread to the countryside, so its looking to Rome as the centre of the Roman Empire had a naturalness which is not easily discernible in the Rome of today. If the argument is from convenience—or even a sense of history—rather than from revelation, then other locations could well be proposed for when a new ecumenical start is made. And if the argument is that Rome is somehow already in possession, then the argument must also be mounted that Anglicans, by sheer force of being Anglicans, are distancing themselves deliberately from Rome, and, if they were to be united with Roman Catholics with a universal primacy built into the foundations of the union, then it might be easier for all if a 'neutral' location for this new kind of primate were chosen.

In short, a universal primacy *could* in principle well correspond to the universal organic 'one-ness' of the body of Christ; but it would have to be proposed on the perceived merits of its proposed functions. It cannot be accepted as revealed from heaven as ecclesiologically necessary—and, we must add, any attempt to attach infallibility to the office would be totally self-destructive. And that is the fourth issue tackled here.

4 Infallibility

The Gift moves its argument step by step towards the infallibility of the 'universal primate,' as a particular, distinctive and (it would seem) integral feature of the primacy. The teaching authority of the whole church is located at the first stage of the argument in the bishops: 'In specific circumstances, those with this ministry of oversight (*episcope*), assisted by the Holy Spirit, may come together to a judgment which, being faithful to Scripture and consonant with Apostolic Tradition, is preserved from error' (para 42).[27] Thus 'the Church may teach infallibly' (para 42).

This task of the bishops is emphasized in para 44: 'The duty of maintaining the Church in the truth is one of the essential functions of the episcopal college.' However, para 47 goes on to state:

Within his wider ministry, the Bishop of Rome offers a specific ministry concerning the discernment of truth...[he expresses the faith of the Church]...It is thus the wholly reliable teaching of the whole

Church that is operative in the judgment of the universal primate… The reception of the primacy of the Bishop of Rome entails the recognition of this specific ministry of the universal primate.

Thus, although General Councils making 'infallible' pronouncements are not ruled out by this doctrine, the capstone of the argument about bishops and their 'infallible' teaching office is that the Pope can actually give expression to their infallible teachings without actually summoning them to a Council.[28]

And, before we come to examine this doctrine, we must remind ourselves that it is not a specifically Roman Catholic statement within *Authority II*— no, *it is the agreed Statement of all the Commission members, Roman and Anglican together*. This adherence by the Anglican members makes it sufficiently serious to warrant a separate chapter of analysing the claim.

7 Assessing the Claim to Infallibility

I wish, as an Anglican bishop, to call these astonishing assertions about the Bishop of Rome into question on three self-evident scores.

a) Is This the Historic Faith, Even on Roman Catholic Terms?

Answer, no—it was imposed by Vatican I, contrary to the whole history of the previous 1800 years of the life of the Christian Church (particularly as evidenced in the early centuries, in the Eastern Churches, in the Churches of the Reformation, and among Roman Catholics themselves before 1870), for reasons which are unsupported in Scripture, and to the very considerable embarrassment of many Roman Catholic historians. It has no claim upon Anglicans, who have hitherto denounced it is as an improper and unsustainable claim, and have conceived themselves as having a duty to resist it.

b) How Does the Claim Here Made Bear Upon the Marian Decrees?

This is a central question for ARCIC Statements on Authority. We have seen above how the only exercise of the papal infallibility has been with the Marian decrees, and how in the ARCIC-1 Statements the issue of infallibility was necessarily bound up with the imposition of the Marian decrees.[29] Yet, here in ARCIC-2, the Marian decrees *have dropped completely out of sight*. The papal infallibility is asserted without any reference to the occasions on which it has been exercised, or the problems which such exercise of it has caused. It has become a wholly abstract kind of doctrine, closed against testing by results, not only because this kind of infallibility is not open to such testing, but also because the results have been suppressed unexamined. Was this omission of the Marian decrees accidental (after *sixteen years* of discussion)? Or was it deliberate, and so deliberate that there is, equally deliberately, not even a hint of an *apologia* for the omission, not a suggestion about how the decrees might relate to the papal infallibility, not a mention even of an intention to hold the discussion in a later statement?

c) Is Then the Infallibility Described Hypothetical Rather Than Actual?

All the statements about the Bishop of Rome look as though they are statements about the existing office-holder and his successors, by virtue of their office. However, that raises the horns of an impossible dilemma—a dilemma never discussed or noticed in the report, yet integral to the whole style of reporting.

The dilemma is simply this:

Either the statements are about the existing Bishop of Rome and the office he holds;

or they are not, but would come into force and require our adherence when some future hypothetical watershed has been crossed.

I wrote in the *Church of England Newspaper* in June 1999 as follows:

The unanimous judgment of the whole Anglican team is that the existing papacy is already the location of an infallible teaching authority. This is put in terms that the Roman Catholics themselves would not have had to accept until 1870, terms which undercut any rationale for separate existence which Anglicans may have thought they possessed.

To this charge, the Bishop of Rochester, Michael Nazir Ali, a member of the Commission, replied as follows:

> One of the tendencies among critics…has been to assume that the Commission…is referring to the Roman Catholic Church as presently constituted. Nothing could be further from the facts…Instead of merely endorsing the present structures of either Church, the agreement looks forward, rather, to a united Church, which has been reformed in the light of the Scriptures…[30]

To this, I in turn replied:

> Now, 'nothing could be further' is itself giving hostages. Later on the Bishop of Rochester explains this:
>
> > …the agreement looks forward, rather, to a united Church, which has been reformed in the light of the Scriptures…
>
> If that were the case, then we would certainly have to read the agreement with different eyes. It is, in fact, that which I looked for, and even expected when I picked up the document. But one has only to turn to paras 41–47, where controlling primacy and papal infallibility are gently but firmly spelled out, to test the Rochester assertions. Every statement about the authority of the Episcopal College, about its focus in the person of the Pope, who holds the see of Peter, and about papal infallibility, is in the historic or present tenses. I cannot find a future verb. I cannot find a hypothetical statement about what 'would be' the case in a future united Church. I cannot even find a conditional sentence, which qualifies or challenges the present standing of the papacy. That which the Bishop of Rochester says is the key to understanding what is said is simply not there…And if it is not there, is it the critics or the Bishop about whose position 'Nothing could be further from the facts'?[31]

Like my episcopal opponent here, all Anglicans are bound to resist the thesis that the Bishop of Rome already possesses these powers—though I think the grammar leaves little room for discussion as what our Anglican participants have signed, so I would cheerfully rest my case there.

But perhaps we ought nevertheless to explore the other horn of the dilemma, namely that, despite the surface meaning of the grammar, all assertions about the Bishop of Rome only refer to such a Bishop of Rome *of the future* 'in a united Church.' Let us suppose for a minute that the Commission did mean that (and that is how the Anglicans were able in good conscience to agree it).

We then have surely to ask: 'In what conditions would the prospect be fulfilled? What union has to occur for the Pope to *become* infallible? What so amazing watershed lies ahead of us that it will, after our two thousand years without an infallible Pope, then in the economy of God finally deliver us the Gift?' What possible conditions could constitute that watershed?

The simplest possible answer in terms of Anglican-Roman dialogue and agreement is that God is waiting for Anglicans and Roman Catholics to unite, and then the Gift will be ours. But in the broad sweep of world Christianity, it is extraordinary that this wonderful prospect of a charism of infallibility is being held back by God solely upon the requirement that the Roman Catholics mop up a relatively small Western Reformation splinter group. Anglican megalomania surely cannot believe that *the* one union needed to bring in this paradise of a totally new gift from heaven of papal infallibility is a union of Rome and Canterbury?

But what is the alternative? Is it that Michael Nazir Ali's future united Church includes *all* the present Christian Churches? If so, then we have traded Anglican megalomania for a kind of ecumenical erewhon. If the prospect of the requisite union is so remote as to be unimaginable, and certainly unbelievable, then what are all the assertions in paras 41–47 worth in practice?

A careful reflection will also reveal one further problem with the assertion that the infallibility belongs to a future united Church. For that *apologia* requires the Anglican team to look the present Roman Catholics in the eye and say to them bluntly: 'We do believe in an infallible Bishop of Rome; but, despite all our indicative moods and present tenses, we are not actually ready to make that affirmation about the present occupant of the see: we are only talking about a future, wholly hypothetical, one.' Now, there is not only no hint of that in *The Gift*, but it is very hard to imagine that the Roman Catholic team would have expressed it the way they do, if they were *sotto voce* having to allow that it gave no credence to the post-1870 actual infallibility that their Church asserts.

So is it possible that the two teams were to commend the Statement to their two Churches *on two mutually exclusive understandings* of what it meant? Well, it is always just possible that, overtly or covertly, they were taking that step. But if so, oh, what has then happened to their transparent and sharp-edged 'yea' which is never 'nay'; and 'nay' which is never 'yea'…?

I find the first horn of the dilemma far more plausible, that is that the statement means what its grammar says. But then the logic of an Anglican 'yea' is submission to Rome as it is; and the conclusion of this commentator is that our 'nay' must be 'nay.'

8   Conclusion

So what is the conclusion of the matter?

Firstly, there should be no edging away from the unchangeable authority of Scripture, an authority which is over all the church. Of course there is a need for leadership, for governing bodies, for administrative organization in any institution. The worldwide character of the church of God has enormous needs in that area. Of course the question of how two worldwide bodies would come together needs draft answers for the two communions to answer. Of course that very properly sets up the possibility of a 'universal primate.' Equally, there is a constant doctrinal formulation going on within the life of the church, a dialogue between the Scripture held in our hands today and the heritage of formulation from the past. Of course that dialogue adjusts to new questions in the institution's life, refining statements from the past, questing eschatologically for right ways to state the faith for the future. But equally, of course, it is wrong to set the people of any age (whether Pope or council or synod or lay disciples) in the false position of being believed to have stated the faith irreformably, thus promoting some secondary formula to rival Scripture itself in its fixity and preservation from error.[32]

I think there is then a need to bring in the issue of consistency between ecumenical dialogues. This was a major theme of the last Lambeth Conference.[33] Anglicans are very keen on promoting the historic episcopate in all dialogues with other Churches, both episcopal and non-episcopal. It looks like the major theological and ecclesiological card we want to play. But *The Gift* is opening up a vastly different set of priorities for us: now the bishops are corporately trustees and guardians of the truth of the gospel, and a universal primate, uniquely equipped by God, can and does articulate that truth in an irreformable form for the health and growth of the worldwide Church. In England we have been involved in conversations of one sort or another in the last decade with the Porvoo Churches, the Meissen Churches, the Reuilly Churches, the Free Church of England, the Moravian Church of Great Britain, the Methodist Church, and (in a slightly indirect way) with the United Reformed Church. I am unaware of any point in any report of any of these conversations where any mention of any powers or any usefulness of any existing or any projected universal primate gets any airing whatsoever. Is this a truth which we hold up our sleeve with a view to springing it on these other unsuspecting partners at a late stage of agreement? Or is it that here our ARCIC members have strayed into a field so alien to Anglicanism that it has never occurred to anyone in any other ecumenical dialogue to put even one foot into that same field?

There is another conclusion, which I adumbrated above. It is somewhat painful to draw, but it goes to the heart of what is said in *The Gift*. It is simply this: that the text is fully compatible with Roman Catholicism, and totally incompatible with anything that most Anglicans have known as Anglicanism. If I believed this text, I would become a Roman Catholic on the spot. I do not understand how signatories of it can take any other view. There remains no possible rationale for being an Anglican in separation from the Bishop of Rome—all critiques, all ground for separation have disappeared. Signing *The Gift* should surely make the signatories accept in their own persons the very 'Gift' they are promoting?

Appendix: How Did It Go So Wrong?

I have suggested above in chapter 4 that, when two 'sides' meet in the way the ARCICs have been composed, then the side which gets the difficult question on the table compellingly sets the agenda.

Perhaps the difficulty of papal authority was inherent in the situation as *the* difficulty to face right from the start. But it was difficult because Roman Catholics could hardly abate an inch from the existing papal claims. Thus those claims became the opening move—the Roman Catholics possessed the white pieces on the chessboard, and had duly played their first move. Every Anglican move thereafter was a reactive one, responding to the claims of the Bishop of Rome. And gradually, in the process and over the years, as the two sides came to enjoy each other and relate easily, the Anglican reaction ceased to be confrontational, but instead moved to first attaching minor qualifications to Roman Catholic statements which they broadly agreed, and finally buying whole tracts of unqualified Roman Catholic statements.[34]

It is this process which, although it got well under way with ARCIC-1, seems to me to have been determinative of the outcome of ARCIC-2. To use the journalistic prose I employed when *The Gift* was first published, the Anglicans were hijacked.[35] And the hijacking lasted that psychological length of time which brings the victims of hijacking to see the world through their captors' eyes. They may then be surprised, when released back into their usual context, to find that outside observers of the hijacking have not moved on in the way they themselves have. To the outsider observers the dynamics of a hijacking are still in evidence, that one crowd has made a show of force and the other crowd has yielded to it. Then, if the captives have adopted their captors' outlook, that will serve them ill once they are back in their normal context.

Deep down, this is not a moral complaint against the Roman Catholic members of the Commission or the way they, almost certainly without artifice, executed their pre-emptive strike. My metaphor is one of doctrinal dynamics not of devious morals! But I have been on many Commissions, and have perhaps dissented on them more often than most of my contemporaries. It is vital in a hijacking, even if one's own associates soften up, still to keep one's previous convictions more or less in place, ready for when all are back in the public arena!

Notes

1   The report was subtitled *Authority in the Church III*, marking it as in sequence with the reports of ARCIC-1, *Authority in the Church I* (1976) and *Authority in the Church II* (1981). However, it is generally denoted here by the shortened title 'The Gift.'

2   A similar process had occurred with *Clarifications*, the disastrous gloss on ARCIC-1 documents which ARCIC-2 produced in 1993, specifically to retouch the language of the Eucharist and Ordination Statements to meet the objections of the Vatican. This had the effect of making Anglican support come from the original documents, while the Pope's new assent was based on this gloss which the rest of us ought to have rejected (if we had been given a chance). It was not circulated to members of Synod, so it proved impossible to get the floor of Synod to insist on a debate. But it is quoted as an Anglican-Roman Catholic agreed document in *Ut Unum Sint*—while, paradoxically, the 1998 Lambeth Conference failed even to mention it in the section report on ecumenism and in the plenary Resolutions arising from it. Was this a conspiracy of silence, or merely sectional amnesia? In *Unpacking the Gift*, Stephen Platten refers to it, perhaps somewhat embarrassedly, on pp 9–10.

3   But actually it may not have been. Those earlier Statements could not agree on some of the crucial issues (see chapter 4 below), and said so. Was there reason to expect that ARCIC-2 would address the same issues—and agree?

4   Sixteen years? Well, the cochairmen say 'five years' (*The Gift*, p 3); but they must have known from the outset of ARCIC-2 in 1983 that Authority and the unfinished agenda of ARCIC-1 were shrieking for attention.

5   One interesting point which I had overlooked is the call by the Pope in *Ut Unum Sint* (1994) for Christians in other Churches to engage with his understanding of his own office and, er, to correct it (see *Unpacking the Gift*, p 9 etc). Any Church seriously attempting to do this would, I suggest, soon find themselves handling exactly the questions addressed in this response to *The Gift*. Certainly, this response meets the Pope at his word.

6   *Unpacking the Gift*, p 60.

7   This was a strongly anti-Protestant nineteenth century handbook for British Roman Catholics.

8   See p 9 for the post-1870 edition.

9   I do, of course, write this without any sense of implicit value-judgments.

10 Torquemada or 'Turrecremata' (1388–1468) was a Spanish Dominican, a theologian who was a member of the Council of Basle, and was created a cardinal in 1439. He actually supported the infallibility of the Pope but opposed the Immaculate Conception (the two issues did not stand or fall together till the nineteenth century); and his treatise *De Veritate Conceptionis Beatae Virginis*, stating his reasons, was published in an English edition (for obvious reasons) by E B Pusey in 1869.

11 Pius IX increased the need to resolve that doubt with his *Syllabus of Errors* (1864); and, although this might possibly have been viewed as protective government rather than new doctrinal definition, it came very near to the decree on the Immaculate Conception in its framing and style. It would be highly embarrassing to Rome today if it were infallible.

12 *Pastor Aeternus* in Denzinger 3074.

13 *Lumen Gentium* (The Dogmatic Constitution on the Church) para 25, a clear echo of *Pastor Aeternus*.

14 'We decree that these Letters…are and shall be always valid and in force…declaring null and void anything which in these matters may happen to be contrariwise attempted…by any person whatsoever by whatsoever authority or pretext…' (*Apostolicae Curae*, last paragraph).

15 It is perhaps worth noting that this olive branch was, arguably, the exact reverse of what Anglo-Catholics then (and often since) have appeared to stand for. They seemed to desire a wholly Roman culture without actual submission to the Pope; this proposed actual submission and yet an enforced retention of an 'Anglican' culture!

16 For the Petrine texts to provide an 'analogy' is actually a surrender of exegetical principle. An analogy illustrates, but does not prove; it provides a possibly convincing likeness between two circumstances, but it does not touch on causal connections between them. As, however, when the props of the Petrine texts have been removed, the papacy can apparently rest secure on what are much flimsier foundations, perhaps the departure of these texts from the argument is of little significance.

17 This short sentence might look as though even in *Authority II* the Anglicans simply accepted that the Pope had protected the church from error down history. But the context shows that the sentence quoted ought to be qualified by 'on occasion,' and the instance quoted is Leo in the fifth century! Nevertheless, the paragraph goes by slow steps towards Vatican I, and the argument is building so that objectors find themselves with less and less ground to stand on.

18 This seems to be exactly the object of a notable book by a notable Roman Catholic member of the Commission, Jean Tillard. He wrote *Le Pape—plus qu'un Pape?* in 1982, and it was translated immediately into English and published the next year as *The Bishop of Rome* (SPCK, 1983). Tillard is the most brilliant re-expounder of traditional Roman Catholic teaching, and on this issue was, of course, totally opposed to ultramontanism. But, as a formally loyal Roman Catholic teacher, he had inevitably to accept the infallibility decree in *some* sense—and he did so.

19 The years 1985–90 were the five years when I was not on General Synod, so I missed the debates which I go on here to report. My much more modest contribution was in Birmingham Diocesan Synod where I opposed the 'sufficient convergence' motion and led the House of Laity to defeat it.

20 *The Truth Shall Make you Free: The Lambeth Conference 1988—The Reports, Resolutions and Pastoral Letters from the Bishops* (CHP for the ACC, 1988) mentions the Authority Statements in the Section report once (on p 139); but they are lost in the plethora of conversations with other Churches, the responding to the other ARCIC Statements, and in the great interest shown in the Lima Statement, *Baptism, Eucharist, Ministry* (WCC, 1982).

21 An 'Explanatory Note' followed the resolution in the Lambeth Report, and this stated that provincial responses from round the Communion had been 'generally positive,' but questions had been raised about primacy, jurisdiction and infallibility, collegiality, and the role of the laity.

22 Granted, as in the Church of England, that the Statements on the Eucharist and on Ministry/Ordination were being hailed as 'consonant in substance with the faith of Anglicans,' the draft resolution on Authority looked very cautious and thus not risky to adopt, even for those with reservations. But I still reckon this was a failure to recognize the danger of the 'direction' being set.

23 The difficulty with this is that Roman Catholics are well able to use 'collegiality' and 'conciliarity' to refer solely to the powers of the episcopate over against the universal primate, without any reference to the laity at all.

24 It was originally published that year in *Catholic International and Origins*, but was made available in English in documents published in Christopher Hill and Edward Yarnold (eds), *Anglicans and Roman Catholics: The Search for Unity* (SPCK, London, 1994) pp 157 ff.

25 Hill and Yarnold, *op cit,* pp 160–161.

26 The Statement has (in line with the conventional, almost indefensible, nomenclature) defined 'local church' as the diocese. Where then are these diocesan synods, with full representative lay participation, in Roman Catholic circles? If such there be, they are not there as part of the constituted structures of the church, but are experimental and voluntary—and, I would judge, pretty rare.

27 This is backed by the tendentious sentence in para 39 that '[At the Reformation] The authority of General Councils was also recognized [by Anglicans].' I call this 'tendentious' because:

   a) Article XXI says 'General Councils…may err, and sometimes have erred, even in things pertaining unto God' and goes on to cite Holy Scripture as that which alone validates the findings of General Councils.

   b) Article VIII, in endorsing the three creeds, rests their authority not on the Councils which (up to a point) agreed them, but upon the basis 'for they may be proved by most certain warrants of Holy Scripture.'

   So *The Gift* is pushing a line virtually contrary to that of the Reformation, which it claims to quote in its favour!

28 Para 47 makes it very clear that the Pope may make such 'wholly reliable' statements in separation from a Council; but, somewhat speciously, it does not use the word 'infallible' about the Pope or about such papal statements. There can, however, be absolutely no doubt but that that is what is intended.

29 See page xxx above, citing *Authority I,* para 24(c) and *Authority II,* para 30.

30 *CEN*, 23 July 1999, p 7.

31 *CEN*, 30 July 1999, p 7.

32 But are not the creeds already in this position? No, I reply, they are not. They are summaries of central features of the scriptural revelation: they are accepted 'because they may be proved by most certain warrants of Holy Scripture' (Article VIII—see note 27 above), not because they emerged from a particular council. And, as secondary formularies, they are still open to the challenge in every generation that they do not express scriptural truth as accurately as they might, even if the challenge is hard then to sustain. That challenging is a proper exercise—but one which it is not open to a Roman Catholic to attempt with, say, the Marian decrees, for they are guaranteed unimprovable *by authority.*

33 See the Section IV Report in *The Official Report of the Lambeth Conference 1998* (Morehouse for ACC, 1999), where Sub-Section 4 (pp 259–265) is entitled 'Consistency and Coherence—Response and Reception.' The Sub-Section report led to the passing of plenary Resolution IV.3 that there should be an Inter-Anglican Standing Commission on Ecumenical Relations. But neither in the discussions of coherence in the report, nor in the detail of the Resolution, is there any hint that the endorsing of a universal primate with the unerring discernment accorded in Roman Catholic circles to the Pope by Vatican I raises any problem for other ecumenical conversations.

34 I do not mean by this that all the drafting was done by Roman Catholics. It may well have been done by Anglicans. But it was done by those who had 'heard' the Roman Catholic position, and were putting it into new, and often quite accommodating, prose.

35 This was in the short passage of arms in the *Church of England Newspaper* in June and July 1999, from which I have quoted on pages 29–30 above.